Until Then

Until Then

A JOURNAL *of* GRIEF, LOSS, LOVE *and* HOPE

Gail Stevenson

Regent College Publishing
www.regentpublishing.com

Copyright © 2014 Gail Stevenson

All rights reserved. No part of this book may be reproduced in any form or by any means, electronic, mechanical, photocopying, recording or otherwise without the written prior permission of the author.

First edition published 2014 by Regent College Publishing
5800 University Boulevard, Vancouver, B.C. V6T 2E4 Canada
www.regentpublishing.com
info@regentpublishing.com

Unless otherwise noted, all biblical quotations are taken from the Holy Bible, New International Version.

Regent College Publishing is an imprint of the Regent Bookstore <www.regentbookstore.com>. Views expressed in works published by Regent College Publishing are those of the author and do not necessarily represent the official position of Regent College <www.regent-college.edu>

ISBN 978-1-57383-511-4 (pbk.)

Cataloguing in Publication information is on file at Library and Archives Canada.

Cover artwork used by permission from Bovard Studio Inc., Fairfield, Iowa

To the loving memory of my husband,
Kenneth Theodore Stevenson

Contents

Preface

My friend Janet said, "You are a writer. Write it all down. Write your thoughts, your feelings and all that you are going through for the benefit of someone who may one day find themself in a similar situation."

But here I was on the edge of tragedy, and everything within me was being assaulted. How could I possibly write in this quagmire of pain, and why would anyone want to read any of this? When my husband received his verdict of death, the words sounded both surreal and unbelievable. I felt a strange and terrified detachment to this awful thing that was still a stranger in our midst, binding us like a vice that would hopefully release soon.

Yet Janet knew what she was saying. She had lost her beloved husband on the eve of Christmas three years earlier, so she knew what it was like to have your world ripped apart and the ground shift under your feet. She understood this gut-wrenching agony that leaves you breathless and emotionally impotent. It was only because of her personal journey that I even entertained such a thought and eventually decided to do it.

However, my story involves more than just two people. It is also a story of how God met the two of us in the midst of our circumstances and walked with us through our pain and suffering. It is a tender commission to write something so personal, so vulnerable in its fragile beauty, and at the same time remain honest and real in the midst of heart-wrenching pain. So, like the prophet Jeremiah, I felt compelled to record the course set before me.

> Set up road signs;
> Put up guide posts,
> Take note of the highway,
> The road that you take. (Jeremiah 31:21a)

This story is not an intrusive look into the personal but rather a glimpse into my heart and the heart of God. Ken and I were blessed with a beautiful love story from the first time we met until the last moments we had together, and I feel it is still happening even though he is gone and I am alone. He will remain forever in my heart. As I write, I pray that I will remain faithful to my purpose, which is to honour my God, my husband and my family.

Part I

Our Story

Every story has a once upon a time. So, sharing our journey as we walked through the valley of the shadow of death is to share our love story, too, and to tell of our family and the many people whose influence and stories became woven into the tapestry of our lives.

My story began with a very happy childhood. I didn't know anything else, and so I assumed that this was the way everyone lived, but I was deeply blessed. My parents experienced the Great Depression, and during my youth, in the 1940s and 50s, we lived through the Second World War. There were years of severe deprivation mixed with fear of the unknown and the unexpected. After the war, I asked my mother if there would be any more newspapers published. When she asked why I would ask such a question, I replied that now that there was no war, I could not imagine what news there would be to report. That was how profound the war had been. Although I was aware of the devastation, the horror of lives lost, and the suffering, my parents were always so full of love and so present in my life that my personal world felt secure, and life marched on.

In my growing years, and at that time in history, certain cultural norms were observed in our society. There was a code of moral conduct that everyone followed, so we were free to go out with many different people, to attend parties and dances, to have a wide circle of friends and acquaintances. Tradition and parental discipline kept us within moral bounds.

In the summer of 1953, I had just turned seventeen and was about to embark upon the season of being a debutante before entering my last year of high school. It was at that time that I met Ken, though it was through a friend of my parents and not in my usual social circle.

Colonel Griffin, whom I knew through my parents as well as through my years of competitive riding, was a retired colonel in the Canadian army. He was also a graduate of the Royal Military College (RMC) in Kingston, Ontario. So it was not strange that he would call my mother and propose that I entertain two young RMC cadets one Saturday afternoon. The two cadets were stationed in Chilliwack for the summer and had been conscripted to help in the planning of the annual ex-RMC cocktail party. Colonel Griffin, well known for his gracious hospitality, had offered to host them for the weekend. He requested that I drive these young men around Stanley Park and then stop somewhere for afternoon tea. My cousin was visiting from California, so she completed the foursome. My mother had accepted on our behalf, and although it sounded like a dull afternoon, out of respect for the colonel and love for my mother, I agreed.

I am embarrassed to remember that I stayed upstairs in my bedroom until I heard them arrive. If I was required to spend the whole afternoon with two young men I had never met, I would at least make sure I was paired with the taller of the two. Because I am five feet seven inches tall, I felt there was good reason for my theatrics. I stood upstairs listening as my mother welcomed them and introduced them to my cousin. I then attempted to float down the stairs, giving myself enough time to do a quick survey of the two cadets. Ken was definitely taller, so I went to his side. What I did not know for quite some time was that my entrance, which must have irritated my mother, deeply impressed Ken. He told me much later that he fell in love at that moment and said to himself, "This is the woman I want to marry!"

The afternoon was sunny, pleasant and perhaps a bit overwhelming. We did not see each other again until two weeks later when Ken picked me up and took me to the fete. Somehow, there was no doubt that I was to be his date. All that summer we saw each other as much as possible in spite of the obstacles of limited transportation and money. At the end of the summer, Ken returned to Ontario. From then on, our courtship comprised mainly correspondence, as Ken was not stationed near Vancouver again. The following summer he did his final rotation in Dundurn, Saskatchewan. I sent him a birthday card to mark his special twenty-first birthday. I found out much later in our marriage that I was the only person who had remembered his birthday. To this day, that still breaks my heart!

&

In spite of a long-distance courtship of less-than-satisfactory letters, and with no telephone because of the expense, our relationship continued. It had challenges, since Ken was a shy young man steeped in military life. When it was time for Ken to graduate from Military College, he invited me to attend the graduation ceremony and Military Ball. This was a lovely invitation, but I had never travelled further than Victoria, so I knew it was completely out of the question. My father made it quite clear he would not allow it. I was relieved in a way, because having to deal with the complexities of it all made me quite fearful. My mother, however, had obviously seen something in Ken that I was not mature enough to fully appreciate. She must have had some serious conversations with my father behind closed doors, because before I knew it, she began to create possibilities for this journey to happen. It was arranged that I would fly to Toronto and stay with my father's cousin, who was the attorney general of Ontario, and his family. After my visit with them, I would be put on a plane to Montreal, where I would be met by, and stay with, the Stevensons, none of whom I had ever met.

When it was all decided and the plans in place, my mother made sure I had all the right clothes for the formal and special occasions that I would attend in both Toronto and Kingston. It was election time in Ontario, and I was to be included in numerous political events, dinners and receptions where clothes and etiquette were very important. There were special shoes and handbags, long white kid evening gloves, shorter ones for less formal occasions, hats and outer wraps, and on and on went the list. And then there was the main event—the Military Ball. This was a white-tie event, and so my debutante dress was carefully packed for the occasion. I remember being taught how to pack my clothes properly, because I had a fairly extensive wardrobe and some of my dresses had full crinolines. It was an art to organize them so that when I arrived, everything would be in perfect condition and ready to be worn with minimal concern.

It had been arranged that after I arrived in Montreal, Ken's family would drive with me to Kingston and chaperone me through the whole event. This provided me with such a secure safety net that I now had great freedom to enjoy living in this beautiful dream.

My falling in love was more gradual than Ken's, but when it happened, it was just as solid and just as committed. Before I returned home to Vancouver, we made an unofficial commitment to be married, but first Ken had to complete his degree at McGill and I would go to business school. Looking back, I realize that this training gave both of us the practical tools that would hold us together as business partners all our lives.

The day that Ken took his degree from McGill University, he headed west with his friend Colin Campbell, who had gone through RMC and McGill with Ken. As neither had any money, they drove Colin's second-hand car non-stop to Alberta, which was Colin's final destination. Ken then took a flight to Vancouver and stayed with my parents until he found a job and a place of his own. Our courtship became more serious and intense, as we now lived in the same city. It was a life-changing summer.

On a sunny Saturday afternoon on June 22, 1957, we were married at St. Paul's Church in the West End. I had just turned twenty-one, and Ken would turn twenty-four the following month. We chose to be married on the same day and in the same church as my parents had twenty-eight years before.

Looking back, I can see the hand of God upon everything, and I also see the deep influence my parents had on both our lives. I will never stop being grateful for my parents' strong commitment to marriage, to love and to family, which we all richly benefited from. They taught both Ken and me that true community and real relationships are not formed in the big moments, but rather in all the daily little steps, the shared experiences, the ups and the downs. We learned that it is the collection of littleness that makes the big things shine. My parents also taught through example the power of loyalty, trust and commitment, and that sometimes things that appeal at first may be nothing more than a façade. I knew that it was incredibly important to be true to who you are and what you believe in, which may at times be a lonely road but will always be a true path.

∽

Ken and I began our married life in an adorable little rented house in the Kerrisdale area on Larch Street. It was like a miniature English cottage. Never in my life have I been happier than I was in those beginning years of our marriage. We rented that little house for five years, and in that time we learned how to be a couple, how to enjoy a simple and ordinary life, which created a good foundation for the times that were to follow. We had our first child, David, and then, at the birth of our second child, Anne, we started the construction business. Our newly formed business office was housed in our home. Ken had his office in the basement and I used the kitchen for my office space. It was all a bit crowded but somehow it worked, until that fateful morning when Ken was seriously injured in a car accident while driving to pick up the mail at the local post office. He was hit in an intersection by a speeding car. He sustained head injuries that took him out of commission for nearly a year. Now we had two children, no income, a newly formed business, and he was out of the game. What to do? There were two options. We could let the company go, as it was still very new, and hope for the best later on, or I could run it and try to keep it going. I chose the latter. For nearly a year, I ran the business with the foreman in the field, and together we managed to keep things moving forward. As Ken slowly recovered, he began to bid on contracts, and gradually we were back in full-running business again.

Several years later, we were able to purchase our own home on Maple Street. We moved the business into an office area nearby. The next five years brought the gift of another child, Evelyn, but were also fraught with challenges and medical issues, especially when I suffered from meningitis. We were both working horrific hours. Ken worked seven days a week, and most days were very long. During these years I had several au pair girls, some of whom were more dedicated than others, but they were another set of hands that made it possible for me to work in the evenings. They would help me get the children bathed and into bed, and then I would drive up to the office to work until nearly midnight.

In these years we had to learn to communicate in ways that we had never experienced before. It is hard to be present for each other emotionally and physically when you are constantly exhausted and overworked, and often not healthy. We had to learn what our priorities really were and how to be a family in the midst of so much pressure. Ken's youngest brother came to live with us for a time after their father died, so our lives were even fuller and more challenging. Yet, in spite of all this we managed to have good family times. We continued to work together, learning to love when we didn't feel loving and to listen when we didn't have the energy.

At this exhausting time, we were dealt a devastating blow. Our home sustained a major fire, where we lost basically everything we owned. Once more we faced the challenge of beginning again. But we did, and through the help of my family we found an old farmhouse that we could rent while we built our new home in the Southlands area. A little over a year later, we moved into what we all remember as the "family home." It sat on two and a half acres of land and was the centre of all our lives. Ken and I each had a horse and the children had a pony. We had dogs, cats, chickens and ducks. We held dances and parties, and every Saturday the children invited their friends to come and spend the day. Ken became Master of the Hunt, and he and his horse went off riding to the hounds all throughout the hunting season. We now had a fourth child, Jake, and I had started my own retail business. These were definitely the growing years. It was during this time that we acquired the first piece of our Qualicum property, which was to become our ocean haven. Our summers were always spent there, and all of us feel that this place was and will remain forever home.

෬

Throughout all our married life, we shared so much. We worked together, we raised a family, we had friendships, we travelled, and although at times we were overly busy and financially stressed, we were always rich in relationship. That pattern never changed. In construction, you know how important it is to put in a firm foundation, because everything rests upon it. That is what we did in those first ten years. It was not easy, and sometimes it was very countercultural and socially lonely, but we were always a team.

Later on, after we closed the construction business, Ken went into partnership with Anthony Hepworth. They formed Pennyfarthing Development Corporation, a happy and successful business partnership that lasted for over thirty years. Tony was one of the few people that Ken respected and trusted implicitly.

In June 1979, we had a deep spiritual awakening. Harry Robinson had arrived in our church, and through his presence and his teachings, the Lord revealed Himself to us in a very powerful way. From that moment on, everything we had, all that we did, would be guided and directed by this new compass. Our past, our present and our future began to come together in a pattern of understanding.

As David said in Psalm 139:

> Oh yes, you shaped me first inside, then out:
> You formed me in my mother's womb.
> I thank you, High God—you are breathtaking!
> Body and soul, I am marvelously made!
> I worship in adoration—what a creation!
> You know me inside and out,
> You know every bone in my body;
> You know exactly how I was made, bit by bit,
> Like an open book, you watched me grow from conception to birth;
> All the stages of my life were spread out before you,
> The days of my life were spread out before you,
> The days of my life all prepared before I'd even lived one day.
> Investigate my life, O God,
> Find out everything about me;
> Cross-examine and test me;
> Get a clear picture of what I'm about;

See for yourself whether I've done anything
    wrong—
Then guide me on the road to eternal life.
    (Psalm 139:13–16, 23–24 The Message)

When we allowed God to open our eyes, what a powerful landscape we found in front of us. We could see all the past and the present converge into one path. We discovered that all that is good and all that is holy had been there all along. God had always been there—we were the ones who had not shown up. As God said to Moses in the wilderness, "I will be with you." Once we claimed that truth, we were reassured that His love is from everlasting, and we were transformed.

This new commitment was to be the focus of all our energies, desires and dreams for the rest of our lives. The Lord, whose hand had been firmly upon us long before this took place, had given us a new perspective. None of our work or our business was wasted or lost, it was simply redirected. This was our new identity, individually and as well as a couple. "God affirms us, making us a sure thing in Christ, putting his yes within us" (from *The Message: The New Testament in Contemporary English* by Eugene H. Peterson, 2 Corinthians 1:21–22).

My conversion, which began at a time of great revival in our church, quickly drew me to take courses at Regent

College, a graduate level theological college. And I decided that after twelve years of running my business, it was time to sell my store—another major change. At this time I took on the role of learning pastoral ministry, as well as continuing my education at Regent.

The college has been a source of ongoing learning over the past thirty years. One of my many happy memories at the college was of attending a course with my mother on prayer, given by Dr. James Houston, who began as my teacher and ultimately became my mentor, spiritual director and friend. Ken was also deeply involved with the college, and sat on their board for quite some time. This place of learning was a beacon of truth for us both. As I write, I am still taking courses there.

So it is not strange that this last chapter of our story would begin with a connection to the college. Like the north wind, this chapter arrived without warning, suddenly and violently taking our story in a very different direction. Our happily-ever-after story began to orbit towards the saddest day of my life.

ல்

It began simply enough. Our dear friend Rod Wilson was giving one of his weekend lecture series at Regent College. When he did these back-to-back lectures, he would often stay at our home on the Friday night, as we lived on the UBC campus. We didn't see him until

Saturday morning at breakfast. As we were setting the table and preparing breakfast, Rod said, "You know, Ken, you do not look well at all. Something is just not right. Why don't you go over to UBC hospital after breakfast and let them look at you?"

I confess to having felt irritated with Ken that morning because he was moving so slowly and not communicating how he felt. This was unfamiliar; we were used to sharing everything. He himself might have been confused with the way his body was operating. As there was no defined pain, it seemed too nebulous to take action, but Rod is a compassionate and sensible man not prone to exaggeration. So with a bit of reluctance, we went.

It was a slightly grey day but free of rain, and there was virtually no traffic, so the drive over was uneventful. The emergency room at the Acute Care Hospital is not as intense or busy as the larger Vancouver General Hospital, so Ken was admitted quite quickly. He went in by himself and I waited in the waiting room. Before long, I was invited to come and sit with him as they did blood tests and routine workups. We were both quite sure that he was probably low on iron and we would be home for our mid-morning coffee. I was completely peaceful. There was absolutely nothing to indicate any need for fear or panic, but slowly the tests became more extensive, and then x-rays were called for.

During the endless waiting, an unknown emotion was escalating, and I suddenly felt the need to call our children. Jake was away, and I thought that Evelyn and Mark were on Vancouver Island, but I called them anyway. It turned out they were in Vancouver. Evelyn said they would come, but I said we were fine: I just wanted to know they were there. However, when she insisted on coming, I was relieved that I was not going to be alone. Something deep down in me was beginning to hear a sound I didn't like—the ring of fear.

They took x-rays, which ruled out any problem with Ken's spleen, but they firmly suggested that we meet with a hematologist on Monday morning. We tried normalizing everything, which is the natural way of coping and moving through the unknown. There was still no real panic or concern. He was fine, maybe a bit tired, but who wasn't? As a post-heart-attack patient, I felt I knew a lot about fatigue. We regarded this as a minor hiccup in life and thought all would be well.

So it came as a surprise to receive a phone call Monday morning from Vancouver General Hospital to say they had an appointment for us with a hematologist the next day. On our way to the hospital, we talked about what might have expedited this quick appointment and decided it was probably a combination of good medicine and our son-in-law Mark being one of the surgeons at the hospital. The specialist felt that it would be wise to have a bone biopsy. Nothing to fret about, just a conclusive test to rule out anything serious. We returned to the hospital on Friday, and the procedure was done in an ordinary room where I was allowed to stay. Everyone was very kind.

On Monday morning, the hospital called to ask us what time that day we could come in and meet with the specialist. Were we on alert? Yes, but although the concern was high, we still thought the problem was treatable. Preventative medicine was all we could think of. We wondered what the "it" was that they had found. "Well, maybe it is leukemia," I said on our way to the hospital. "You know, the kind that is really low grade. Joanne's mother has had it for years, and they have been able to treat it effectively with oral chemotherapy. She seems absolutely fine." We were sure that although this would not be pleasant, it would be manageable and we would deal with it. We carried a quiet optimism that we knew would take us on a different path, but a path with a future that we could cope with.

In the doctor's office, our optimism slowly faded: something had dulled the hopeful face we wished to see. For a moment, there was silence, like a taut canvas awaiting the stroke of a brush. What was the painting going to look like? What would we see? The doctor's opening was brief and to the point. "I never expected the results we have received," she said. "It appears that you have Acute Myelogenous Leukemia. I am so sorry." We listened to each word, watched each stroke of the brush. The image emerging was dark and formidable. This impossible object, this horrific picture, this reality, this altogether too much, too big, too horrible thing was not only an assault to the senses but an attack on our hearts. It jarred itself into the very essence of our souls.

The angst of the image hung before us. Her words, expressing both professionalism and concern, were drowned out by the strangled gasping erupting from my being. Like Vesuvius, the pressure and power of pain kept exploding, over and over again. Everything was falling, crashing off this ledge of horrible truth, gushing and flowing in hot, heavy streams of lava pain.

Ken, the steady one, the reasonable voice, the quiet strength, the commander-in-chief against this assault, asked the sensible question: "Is there any treatment?"

"Unfortunately with this, there is no treatment. The malignant cells reproduce at random, taking huge leaps that are impossible to get ahead of or even come near. Sadly, there is nothing that can be done."

"How much time have I got? What is the life expectancy?" asked Ken.

"Three to six months" was the answer.

Here was my beloved husband, calmly listening to his death sentence, acquiring facts and figures, while I was drowning in the absurd knowledge of the surreal and losing all sense of direction. My worst nightmare was being discussed—and Ken was asking for guidance and directions. The doctor explained that we would be assigned to a specialist who would walk with us through the rest of this journey. Soon, the meeting was over.

Just as we were leaving the doctor's office, a question occurred to me: "Did you receive the results from the bone marrow test on Friday?" Her reply was gentle and compassionate, in stark contrast to her antiseptic office. "Yes, but how could I have called you and left you with that news over a weekend?" Her genuine caring made us pause in the doorway, but then the tide of reality we were now riding, this pull of life, told us we had to move on.

We made an appointment with the new doctor and then walked out of the hospital, into the parking lot, into the car, and drove home in silence. Shock, horror and disbelief reigned. Surely there had been a mistake. But the hard truth was that this was real, and somehow we had to find a path forward and through it all.

Ken remained the steady one, the calm one who took control. I tried to adjust by not getting in the way. We made coffee and sat as we always did, in the same place, doing the same things that form ritual. Over muffins and coffee, he said, "We need a plan. We need to start with the first thing that we have to do. Who do we call first and how do we begin?"

We called Evelyn and she came immediately. He spoke, I sat and listened. He told her quietly and caringly, using words more informative than emotional. He displayed empathy and a slight apology for upsetting us all. She signed on; he never had to ask. On that Monday at noon, on the eighth day of February, 2010, the team was formed. In that moment, an unfamiliar and uncharted journey began.

Part II

My Journal, 2010

After we had established how we would navigate this journey, I pondered Janet's suggestion to keep a journal. I was already emotionally exhausted and was trying to deal with my own health issues. This, combined with the unknown mountain of challenges, made life all the more daunting and frightening. I was also mindful that this was Ken's journey and the need for privacy was very important. My main concern was to care for him, to love and guard him, as well as to protect the intimacy of this journey.

Yet it was Ken who said to do it. "Write for as long as you can," he said. "It may be a blessing to someone else."

I had no idea what a journal would look like, but I felt the hand of God nudging me on. Perhaps it would put some purpose and meaning into a morass of pain. Slowly I became aware that by observing how God directed me along this uncharted path, I would discover the consolation of His presence.

Over the years, and through many of my life experiences, I have learned that the pen writes me. Many times, my own words have become the teacher I needed to discover the journey of my heart. So I began to journal, and through my writing I discovered that I was telling God how it really was. I saw the freedom that comes with being totally honest. I began to learn that when we risk not being in control and invite God into the mess, the pain and the unknown, He not only meets us but gathers our gripping rawness of grief and slowly turns fear into love. We may not choose this journey, but we can choose how we are going to live through it.

What follows are the facts and emotions as I experienced them, things I would never have believed, things both horrific and holy. I wrote this in faith and for my own reasons of understanding. But more importantly, I wrote this to honour my husband and our God—our God who led us step by step all the way through and created in me the desire to echo the words of the Psalmist:

> I will sing of the Lord's great love forever;
> with my mouth I will make your faithfulness
>   known
> through all generations.
> I will declare that your love stands firm for-
>   ever,
> that you establish your faithfulness in heaven
>   itself. (Psalm 89:1–2)

❧

Monday, February 15, 2010

In the week since we got the news, we have moved at such an incredible pace that it makes my head spin. In just seven days, we have shut down all Ken's bank accounts and his credit card and have placed all assets into my name. My words are ridiculously simple compared to the work that has been done.

We have notified all the family, the church family, our friends and everyone who would be hurt by hearing it from someone else or we would feel terrible at not letting know. We are all vulnerable to pain, loss and death. In hearing of another's pain, we find ourselves in that person's story, in some small way, and briefly experience our own mortality. It is amazing to me to realize that the following words have circulated around the world and, tragically, created a great deal of pain for many.

> It is with a heavy heart and great sadness that I write these words to you. We have just heard from the hematologist that Ken has Acute Myelogenous Leukemia. Sadly, it is not treatable, and he has been given between three and six months. At present, he is feeling quite well, although he fatigues easily. Because his immune system is so compromised, infection has become a deadly enemy for him right now. He would so love to be with those he enjoys and loves, but being in contact with people is, alas, not an option. So we find ourselves in a new and strange place, but at the same time we are holding tightly to the promises of hope that we

have in the Lord, and in the comfort and strength that we have and take from your friendship and prayers. Right now, because of the need for quiet and for the sake of the family, emails are probably easier than phone calls. We thank you for the gift of your strength, friendship and prayers.

All love and blessings,
Gail

Wednesday, February 17

The emails keep coming, each filled with love and caring thoughts. It is a full-time job just keeping up with them. It is *so* much kinder and easier to receive emails than to talk on the phone or have to write notes to people. I find the emails a great gift and a wonderful connection.

Yesterday, we saw the specialist in what is known as AML, or Acute Myelogenous Leukemia. It always amazes me that the language of medicine is as unfamiliar as the language of a court room or business office or other arena you are not usually engaged in. It isn't until your feet hit the pavement that you realize that this is not the culture in which you normally live, or would ever want to live. But it is here that we now reside, and somehow we must find a home in this strange land with a language we don't want to hear. And yet, here we have also found compassion, care and a great human respect, which is a kindness to the assaulted heart.

The doctor said that Ken's genetic base (a term far too simplistic) is strong enough to consider a light dose of chemotherapy. The dosage would be a tenth of what would be given in aggressive treatment. It will not cure him, but might extend his life slightly. I find this news somewhat like a death sentence that might be delayed if your behaviour is really good, but the end result remains the same. Naturally, Ken is keen to do it; if he feels nauseous, he can stop and nothing will be lost in the adventure. But is it a false hope or a positive step forward? I don't know. One thing I do know is that he is the love of my life, and I would do anything for him and agree to whatever he wishes. Oh, that I could be the one making this decision about *my* life; oh, that I was the one with the stamped ticket to Heaven; oh, that it wasn't him!

Tomorrow we meet with Dan Gifford, the associate rector of our church, to talk about where we are in all of this. I have written, at Ken's request, an outline for his funeral service. I am happy with the results of this labour only because it pleases him. After all, this is his service and he needs to be a part of it. The good thing about a gift of time is that you get to be part of the planning: it is *your* last farewell, instead of everyone else's often-cobbled thoughts and ideas.

Exhaustion is my constant companion, and I am going to have to learn to temper this if I am to stay well. I am continuing with my fitness instructor, who is such a sensitive guy for one so young. It is our common goal to make me as strong as possible. As we experience this trauma, the 2010 Winter Olympics are being held in Vancouver, and I feel that I am training for my own little Olympics—except for me, gold is to lose.

We have planned a family weekend at Qualicum. I needed to send a letter outlining all that we had discussed individually, because I felt that it was important to be able to speak into each moment with clarity and understanding. If I have learned anything in this life, it is that we assume that everyone hears and understands as we do. But even your children, those dear ones closest to you, are often the ones who hear things so differently. They are also in this strange land, after all, and our understanding of the local dialect is different for each of us. So I wrote:

Dearest ones,

It is your father's good wish that you, his children—which includes you, Donald, as he has always seen you as a son—would join us at Qualicum on the weekend of February 26. In spite of the sad situation in which we now find ourselves, there is great joy and comfort in being able to all be together.

Because of the nature of Dad's condition, we have been given a rare gift of time to celebrate and remember all that is good and all that we have shared as a family. What we have had will continue, and where we are now, although exquisitely painful, is also a holy and blessed time. We want to value this time and one another, and celebrate with Dad all that he loves best, which is, of course, his family.

Even though this may seem inappropriate, and even trite, we have two birthdays to celebrate as well, David's fiftieth and Jake's fifty-fifth. It gives your dad a great sense of joy to be able to celebrate and remember with you, so we shall go forward with these moments of celebration. On a practical note, due to Dad's possibly changing physical condition, we should probably have dinners at our house at an unseemly early hour each day, and then perhaps just play the rest by ear. Most important is time, and he looks forward to spending this both individually and collectively with our family.

My mother heart is aching for you, my dear children, as I remember all too well how it felt to lose your grandfather. He was so dear to us all, but here we are, these many years later, remembering him in love and with a smile in our hearts. So we know we will be blessed with the same freedom and gift of memories. Sadly, this would be too much for Anne emotionally, so we have to keep it as quiet as possible so as not to create any undue pain for her. She will spend time with Dad, and I know that you are sensitive to her need to be protected from this.

We both look forward to all ten of us being together again. We send you our love and wrap our arms around your aching hearts. We remind you again how dearly you are loved and how blessed we are to have you near us!

Love and hugs in abundance,
Mum

They are all coming, and there is something quite wonderful about being able to plan this time together. I feel enormously proud of our children as I hear them caring for each other, concerned for how the other feels or is going to feel, and of course for their great love for their dad. Another of those great blessings that we fail to see when we get so caught up in the enormity of the moment.

MacGregor, our Westie, is not feeling well. He has been sick to his stomach, and today I had to entice him to eat by placing carrots in his food after the meal had sat there most of the day. I will have to careful not to let him become too sad. I love his little sensitive and caring heart. Wouldn't it be lovely if people loved each other that much!

Thursday, February 18

Bad morning. MacGregor isn't well. We made an appointment with the vet at noon, right after the groomer. We were told he has an abscessed anal gland, which required treatment and medication. He is at home now after a $300 day at the clinic, antibiotics, and instructions to give his bottom warm compresses every few hours. Am I happy to do all this? Oh yes! I almost lost it, thinking he was really sick and I might lose him. That would have been the straw that breaks, the final breath that shuts you down, the last bullet in my arsenal of strength. Praise be to God he is now home and well!

Today we met with Dan. He arrived at 2:30 p.m. as planned and stayed over an hour, which was helpful and meant a great deal to Ken. We talked about death and dying and about the funeral service. Then he did the healing service with the anointing of oil. It was all good.

It is evening. Much has happened and much was done, and tomorrow is full to the brim with appointments and responsibilities. I am bone-tired and about to prepare for bed.

Tuesday, February 23

Today was full. MacGregor went back to the vet, a happy event, and then Harry Robinson came for a visit, which was precious and sad. After he and Ken had had their personal time, Harry went through the service for the sick from the Book of Common Prayer. I have never known Harry to be anything but gentle and compassionate. As I listened to him read the service and to our voices doing the responses, I was mindful that in the midst of our lives, the constant and orderly rhythm of God's word and our response is like the ocean and its tides: ever moving, ever full, ever cleansing and life-giving. We are not the rhythm; we are just part of the dance. It is very comforting. Harry thinks he might get to Heaven before Ken, and it was dear to see these two old and good friends discuss their pending journeys with the natural anticipation of a joyful future. They were quiet and respectful of the enormity of it all, and gentle with each other. It was an amazing time.

The clock man came to adjust the clocks, and I had to tell him why it was so important to have everything working. He is a sensitive man and worked hard to make the two clocks work—the old grandfather clock in the family room and Mother's beautiful antique French porcelain clock, which has been moved to the living room to ensure it is in perfect balance. He wouldn't let me pay him, and left in such a calm and gracious way. Unfortunately, within two hours both clocks stopped working, and I felt like giving them both a good spanking!

At six o'clock Jake arrived, and Heather, his wife, followed about fifteen minutes later. It was good that Jake had some time with his dad first. When Heather arrived, she and I sat in the living room and talked while Dad and Jake completed their conversation. The first time you see someone after hearing news like this is the most difficult. You experience a deep-down fear: fear of what you have heard, fear of not being able to cope, and fear of the unknown, which is perhaps the greatest fear of all. Once you have jumped over that hurdle, the journey, though rough and uneven, becomes your new landscape and the walk through it gives you some sense of what may lie ahead. Each new time is hard, hard on us who are bearing it and hard on those who have to find their place within it. Then, somehow, the unfamiliar becomes familiar and the steps forward become less terrifying.

Wednesday, February 24

Today we leave for our last trip to Qualicum. Evelyn has taken my car with their dog Sami to catch the early morning ferry. Grandson Hugh has the van, and he is my official driver until David arrives with Ken's car. After getting my hair done, I pick up a prescription for sleeping.

Although I hate the idea of being dependent, I realize that being any more exhausted than I am would not be a good thing. Dear dependable Hugh returns me home where we share a cup of coffee, and then he leaves as David arrives. We are now packed up in the car and ready for the drive to the Boundary Bay Airport.

Sunday, February 28

Today is David's fiftieth birthday, and Thursday was Jake's fifty-fifth birthday. Last night we celebrated our last family dinner: our farewell to Ken and a farewell to all the times that we as a family have celebrated over these fifty-plus years. Evelyn and I planned this very carefully, but when you live with the ramifications of this disease and all the circumstances around it, the plan you make today will become a different plan tomorrow. So we adjusted it many times, but what we were able to have on Saturday was the best of blessings through and through.

The menu, like everything else, was changed and adapted, but this is how it was at the end. Our children arrived at four thirty in the afternoon to have pictures taken with their dad. Then at five o'clock, after everyone had arrived, we did a family photo. Christine, from next door, came over and took the picture. She is aware of what is happening here and has been a gracious tower of strength, and today she made the most beautiful lasagna ever for us all.

Before we went into the dining room, I looked at these dear children of ours standing in front of the blazing fireplace, amidst the glowing candles, surrounded by the many white roses, and I told them what their father had told me not so very long ago. He said that he felt our children were all safe and settled in their lives and he didn't have to worry about them anymore. He mentioned each one by name and why he was proud and peaceful about where they were in their lives. After struggling to tell them this amidst the painful reality, I ended the story with a prayer. I asked the Lord to bless our evening. I asked Him to bless the food we would eat and the words we would speak. I prayed that He would bless our laughter and our tears and every aspect of the time that we would be spending together.

Then Ken, being Ken, decided to say his speech before dinner rather than during the meal as planned, and so he began. He talked about faith, integrity and love. There was both pain and pride in my heart as I listened to the power of his beautiful words. He was occasionally humorous and always loving and poignant. I watched him give his children a powerful legacy that would remain with them for the rest of their lives.

The dinner that followed was exactly the gift it was meant to be. Caesar salad began the meal, followed by an exquisite rack of lamb surrounded by baby vegetables and potatoes, all washed down with vintage wines. But the most priceless gift was the memories shared, stories that brought volumes of laughter and tumbling tears, precious and perfect moments that will continue long after the candles have burned down and the flowers faded. In the midst of such sorrow, we were indeed blessed.

As this day was also for David's and Jake's birthdays, we celebrated with cake and gifts and toasts and genuine joy, because we had been able to embrace all that was good and all that was true before we ever began.

Friday, March 19

It is amazing to me that I could write in such detail about the family dinner. Now that we are back in Vancouver and into our routine of chemo, living and sorting, I am unable to even write my name. What has happened to my energy and my time?

Saturday, March 20

Evelyn and I set off for Talbots at Oakridge to find a black dress for Anne. Evelyn had planned it all, and we were fortunate that the manager, Lila, whose personality is golden, had things ready and waiting for us even though she was to start a much-needed holiday that evening. How blessed is that! The right size is being delivered to the store next week and we can pick it up. We each bought a couple of spring shirts, though it felt eerie, in the midst of the sobriety of death, to prepare for spring and a new season of life.

Saturday, March 27

A week has come and gone, and with it another level of energy. Yesterday, Mark was off duty but went in to check on his surgical patients as well as to read Ken's blood work from the day before. His platelets and red blood cell count were dangerously low. Mark immediately called us and then picked us up, as there was a bed booked at the hospital for Ken to receive transfusions. We spent the day there.

Evelyn and I went for lunch, and then she and Mark left for Qualicum, which they had already delayed. Ken and I returned home a little before six, exhausted and not quite aware that we had walked a little too close to the edge of the mountain. He could have had a massive bleed, and nothing would have stopped it. There will have to be some adjustment done on who is in charge here. Thank God for Mark, and also for Evelyn for alerting her brothers and those that needed to know. Jake was out of town but kept in touch via his cell phone, and she let him and David know we were fine. I do not want our children to have the burden of being responsible for our every faltering move. Neither of us slept well.

Today we are muddling along. I went to Talbots and picked up Anne's dress, and then did a few groceries. We had coffee, lunch and long sleeps, and now it is time to prepare dinner. Hopefully, the Lord will grant us a quiet night where the busyness of our wearied minds may rest in Him and find peace.

Tuesday, April 6

It is hard to believe that it has been nine days since I last wrote. In that time, we have celebrated Palm Sunday, Holy week, Good Friday and Easter Sunday, all deeply meaningful and significant to both of us. Now, as I sit and think upon that time, I realize that it was packed with tenderness, grief and celebration, and perhaps, in the midst of it all, a deeper sense of acceptance and understanding.

This was the first time we had not been included in the services and the observations of all that is involved with Easter. We were mindful of the special significance of this Palm Sunday, of the sacrificial lamb being brought into the City of Jerusalem, of Passover and the pending Holy week. After Maundy Thursday came Good Friday; we stayed home and only took the dogs for walks. We observed the silence and heard the story anew, and lived it in our hearts.

I am writing about Easter Sunday some three weeks later, as much has happened and my fatigue prevented me from writing.

On Easter Sunday, we observed the Lord's Supper together. Several years ago, on a trip to Spain, I purchased a beautiful white cotton table runner from a market stall in Madrid. Spaced equally within the runner were three cutwork lace crosses. I laid this upon the mahogany coffee table, added two silver candlesticks and the wooden Jerusalem cross that I had purchased in Israel, and then set the chalice and paten in place. I had prepared the service, which took exactly an hour, and never in my memory have I experienced a deeper sense of the holy or sacred than I did within that hour. We offered the bread and wine to each other, and in these moments Christ was not only with us, He was so deeply in our midst that the very silence held a reverent sound. That evening I cooked a simple but special Easter dinner, which we shared, and as the day brought itself to an end, we were mindful of how Christ had met us so deeply this day. I will always remember that Sunday—so special, so meaningful, so profoundly sacred. We were deeply blessed.

Wednesday, April 28

It has been three weeks since I last wrote. I am exhausted and so much has happened. Ken has not done anything in the way we expected, and it feels like we can do nothing except witness his decreasing energy and increasing fatigue.

We have had two emergency runs to the hospital, both nightmares. God willing, they will not be repeated. He had two terrible bouts of intense pain that morphine did not touch, and it took a long time to stabilize him. Each time there was no diagnosis, as they could not find the source of the pain. It would hit him in either the stomach or the back and then travel around his chest and abdominal area until he was literally writhing. He would then throw up and rock in the agony. Each visit lasted four to five days, and he had to be kept in an isolated room where endless tests and medications were administered.

Now we are home again, simply living each day as it comes. He is more and more distanced from his world. That is to be expected, but as I observe him removing himself, it brings me closer and closer into my own pain.

Saturday, May 7

Today, I think I have had to accept that the husband I had is now the child I am caring for. At times I am an enemy, at times an angel, depending on his mood and the time of day. I am emotionally and physically exhausted. His needs are becoming greater as the illness takes over more and more. It crowds out reason and understanding, leaving confusion and exhaustion in its devastating wake.

Food has become an enormous problem, as his taste buds are off and his appetite has waned to a difficult level. But the hardest part is the ever-changing emotions—one minute I have him, the next minute I don't. I cry, I weep, I exhaust, but then I think, "Well, he is still able to walk and talk and eat, so praise be to God!"

We had two more trips to the hospital. Earlier this week, we went into emergency at UBC so they could insert a catheter, because voiding has become an issue. Due to his prostate surgery, there has been a buildup of scar tissue, making insertion impossible, so Mark sent us to a specialist in urology at VGH. They did a scoping and issued a different antibiotic, in case that was the problem. For the moment, things are under control. Yesterday, we went for a day trip for two units of blood.

Today we are dealing with extreme fatigue. But hey, the house is polished and clean and the laundry is piled high after being washed and ironed and the bed is made and the bathing is done and there is enough food for today and how blessed is that!

Sunday, May 9

It is Mother's Day. One of our customs as a married couple is to give each other our gifts early in the morning on festive occasions. Even at Christmas time, Ken and I exchange our main gifts on Christmas Eve. Today, I prayed that none of the children would call and wish me a happy Mother's Day. He was too sick and would have felt awful not to have remembered. The last thing I wanted for him was unnecessary pain. I made breakfast and brought it into him on the bed tray, all the while treating this as an ordinary day. I found him sitting up in bed and looking quite happy. I sat down beside him and he asked, "Are you not going to open your Mother's Day present?" There, sitting beside him on the bed, was a beautifully wrapped box with a card. I was completely taken aback. How could he have done this? How had he remembered? "Open it," he said, and he was as excited as a little boy. I had a hard time with this, especially the card in which he had written such beautiful words. In the box was a string of exquisite pearls.

All through our marriage—when money was tight, when we were struggling with finances, when there was too much work and too little time, when we were building the construction business and juggling family life with little children—he has been that kind of man. It could be a rose from the garden or pearls of rare beauty, but he always remembers, always says I love you, always makes me feel special. That is what is important. Not the gift but the sentiment, not the financial value but the care and love. That is what makes him so special. In all circumstances and all stages of our marriage, he has been and continues to be caring and loving.

I was overwhelmed. I was also mindful that these pearls were not inexpensive. "How? Why?" was all I could say. I remember his words: "This is the last gift that I am able to give to you, and I wanted it to be something that you would wear and something that was beautiful. Try them on and let me see how they look." I did, and then he said, "Now, wear these to my funeral. Will you put on the suit you are going to wear and let me see how they will look?" I put on my black suit and placed this beautiful strand of pearls around my neck. Then I heard him say, "You look so beautiful. It makes me feels so happy and proud knowing that this is what you will be wearing."

Can you imagine? This is who he is. There is nothing in this story any different from my whole married life. The only difference is that we are not going to do this together—and yet, perhaps we are.

Tuesday, May 11

Yesterday, exhaustion set in once again and I simply couldn't run the race anymore. But with the enormous help and wisdom of my daughter Evelyn, I slept and she coped, and the day went through its normal cycle—and we all survived. By day's end, Ken and I were able to communicate the way we always used to. It was like a fresh sunrise and new air filling the room, as well as my lungs and my heart, transforming every part of our being. For a short time, I was myself again and we were a couple, and all was well in our world.

Today, I see the fatigue coming back, like the mean old Witch of the North. I have learned that it is selfish not to rest when I need to, and that a clean house is not going to keep either of us alive. What I will remember and hold dear to my heart will not be antiseptically clean moments. Oh, how hard it is to trust God with the mess and the fear of the unknown. I trust Him, yet I am learning anew that to let go evokes fear that I may become so unravelled that I will never be myself again. This sacrifice seems beyond my abilities, but the graciousness of the Lord lies in His faithfulness and loving understanding. I will survive in spite of myself. Ken's new journey is going to happen, and where he is going is all ordained. This little bit of order is just my way of coping.

So today, I am going to try to rest and let God be God and prepare for the unknown that will have moments far greater than I can ever imagine. "God's grace is my sufficiency, and His power is perfected in my weakness."

Thanks be to God that in all our moments of despair and weakness, He is making us new in His image!

Friday, May 14

Today we were admitted into the Palliative Care Unit of the hospital. It may or may not be the last time we are here, for only the Lord knows the hour and the place, but we have arrived at a safe place and I am grateful. The last two days came close to a living hell, and I do not want to repeat them ever again.

Saturday, May 15

Jake came by the house in the morning and drove me to the hospital, which I appreciated. Ken was alert and had slept well, and I found the quiet calm of this place a refreshing oasis. Very soon he was back to sleep, and so together we spent the morning in quietness.

All the nurses in this unit are amazing, and it is obvious that it takes a special person to do this kind of nursing care. They are gentle but quiet, and at home with themselves. I am learning again how intuitive we can be to emotion and feelings. As soon as someone comes into the room, you feel their presence. If they are at home with themselves, then you are at home with them. You pick up any resistance, criticism or distaste immediately. Some are more equipped than others for this job, and some are beyond expectation.

We also find we can only handle family and friends who hold us in the place we are in, and love us there. I think we narrow our world for the simple reason that it takes too much energy to be with people who expect us to be someone we are not.

Evelyn came by later, and we went to City Square for a salad lunch around two o'clock. She is a wonderful gift from God, and I am constantly amazed at her wisdom and sense. It is great freedom to be able to talk about what is really happening and to give each other permission to feel the way we do.

It is hard work now, and although the loss of Ken will be a knife in my heart, it is time. All has been said and done, and now we wait in the darkness of the unknown for the light of his new tomorrow. It is hard work, this waiting. Ken's health is such that at one moment he appears to be at the brink of death and at the next he pops up clear, lucid and ready to go! We are changing gears faster than we can drive.

I went home a bit earlier than usual, and I found the quiet and solace of the house cathartic as I tidied and settled myself into a rhythm. I listened to hymns and wept and prayed, and prayed and wept, and then it was bedtime. Ken called from the hospital, all settled for the night, peaceful and full of love, and in that moment there was peace and quiet and a deep sense of holiness. Although apart, we were together.

Sunday, May 16

Like so many days, this one has been unique. When I arrived this morning, Ken was quite disturbed that he had fallen after getting out of bed during the night. His wonderful determination, what has kept him going throughout his life, is now part of the battle he has to face. In his resolve to go to the bathroom without assistance, he fell and urinated over himself. It nearly broke my heart to see what this did to him emotionally. Thanks be to God that he did not break anything, but today he is weak and frail and has slept most of the time.

The Sunday service I had planned, I said by myself, but I put on the hymns, which he heard as he slept. There was deep worship in that room, and Christ was present, holding us both in the palm of his hand and in the shadow of his wing.

When Ken awoke, he said, "It has changed again and I am slipping." We talked about the next stage of giving over, and the acceptance and difficulty of it, knowing that it is an inevitable part of this journey. The beautiful thing is that he no longer has to create the energy to walk or talk or eat unless he wants to, so the place where he is, is exactly where he is meant to be. We are doing this together, and although my heart is breaking, I am aware that there is a host of angels in that room, and what could be empty silence is really holy ground, surrounded and held in place and navigated exactly the way it should be. My problem is that I, too, have to be obedient to the unknown and try not to second-guess this next part of the journey.

As I was preparing to leave this evening, I said clearly to the doctors that I must be called during the night, even if it seems too soon, because that is where I want to be— right with him all the way. I expect to be sleeping at the hospital very soon, but for now I am home, and in a short while I will find my way to bed, alone yet held by Jesus. Ken just phoned, as he has done every evening since being in hospital, and reminded me that God wants me to be strong and do what He has in mind, and that I have a life ahead of me and God is going to bless it. I weep when I see my future without him beside me. What have I to say or write or do that will ever be worthwhile, or even the same? And yet, and yet.

Monday, May 17

Today is my granddaughter Emma's twenty-second birthday, and last night I sent her an email wishing her happy birthday. It is strange to feel so disconnected in my connecting. I care about her deeply, as I do all my family, but the energy to really be there does not exist. I have one thought, one focus, one purpose, and that is Ken. As I was having my breakfast this morning, I wondered how on earth I will ever "do a day" when, by eight o'clock, I had already showered, dressed, made my bed and cleaned my house. What will my days look like and how will I manage when I no longer have my focus on Ken? What will I do and who will I be?

I will be leaving in half an hour for the hospital, and there I will remain until it is time to leave. Nothing else matters, nothing else exists for me right now. It is strange this place I am in, because although I am lost, I am not really lost; although I am deeply sad, I am also comforted; although I am so alone, I am not alone. It is just that sometimes a strange, empty and grief-filled moment hangs like a great droplet of sadness, but with the hand of God I shall overcome. So I begin this day, and as always this day belongs to the Lord, for which I am eternally grateful, for if I had to orchestrate it, it might be a complete disaster!

Tuesday, May 18

This is a new day. I am going to have a sleepover with Ken at the hospital tonight! In a strange and painful way, I am really excited. I have packed two little baskets, one with my dressing gown and slippers, and fresh underwear and another top for tomorrow, and the other with my toiletries and fresh pajamas for Ken. He wants me there beside him now, and I *so* want to be there! Yesterday, he said he was near the end, so most of the day he slept and showed little or no interest in food. Then at five, Mark came in to see him before he left for home. Guess who was all perky and full of chat, with no resemblance to what Evelyn and I had been seeing all day?! However, after a phone call from him in the evening, I knew in my gut that I was doing the right thing. This is where I want to be. Last night before I left, Ken asked me to pray with him. "I only want to hear the words from the Bible and to hear you pray," he said, and so I prayed the service for the dying, as well as other favourite prayers. What else would he want to hear as he enters closer and closer to the kingdom of God? We both found this comforting.

Today at four o'clock, David Short is coming to give him communion. I believe that we are doing things in the right order, but my heart is hurting. As I feel the spasms, I realize I must work with God to keep myself peaceful and centered as we walk through this valley of the shadow of death, knowing that at some point I will have to stay behind and let him go.

Wednesday, May 19

Ken is in a lovely room in a newly constructed pavilion of the hospital. The pavilion was named after its donor, who happens to be Ken's friend and colleague. This afternoon, quite out of the blue, Ken said to me, "I would really like you to write to him and thank him for creating such a lovely place for people to spend their final days on earth. Tell him how much I appreciate his great generosity, and tell him how I appreciate all he has done." Then he told me the name of his friend's personal assistant and where to send the letter.

I said, "Ken, I can't do this, it is too hard. By the time I get home I am exhausted, and this is not an easy thing to do."

"You can do it, you are good with words," he said. "Just write what I said and put it into a letter form. You can do it."

I have to admit that when I returned home this evening, I was not prepared to write this letter. Once you walk through your own front door, the enormity of the situation you are living in falls over you like a heavy blanket, and fatigue plays the trump card. I was so exhausted that the thought of climbing the stairs to the office, creating an appropriate letter, and doing the research for sending it, was beyond me. But I did it, and I will mail it on my way to the hospital tomorrow morning. I don't think it ever entered his mind that I would do otherwise.

Friday, May 21

It is now exactly one week since we arrived at the Palliative Care Unit at the Vancouver General Hospital. I still see it for the lovely gift it is: quiet, tranquil, a gentle place to close one's life. This is the first long weekend before the summer months, and many people have plans, so hospital life tightens up. Surgeries only happen on an emergency basis, making it even quieter for the next three days.

Ken has had enough of this mortal life, and things have changed once again. I am well aware that there are times when people need permission to die. I know this both academically and practically. When my mother was dying, I was able to hear this and we were able to communicate in ways we both understood. Yet here, in this moment and this situation, I completely missed the obvious. Maybe it was because it came in a way I did not recognize, or maybe it appeared to be such a negative instead of a positive. Here I was fighting to keep him alive, to feed him, to do anything that would bring comfort and peace, and I never thought, I could not see, that I was missing the one thing he was asking of me—to stop doing what I was doing. Even when he said, "I am all done," I did not realize what he was asking me to do. Up until this point, I had cajoled and begged him to eat, to drink, anything, just eat! I had dreamt up every possible thing that might be appetizing, had cooked endless things that might please his palate, anything to encourage him to eat, anything to bring nourishment to his body. "Eat or you will die" had become my mantra, and now it was cruel, but I couldn't see that.

I don't think I ever did see it, really. Somehow, I think God just put the words into my mouth and I heard myself saying, "You know, Ken, you don't have to eat anymore." It was not long after that that he asked the palliative care doctor to come into his room. He asked her, "Do you know how wise my wife is? Do you know what she just told me?" The doctor was a skilled and wise woman, and so she inquired what I had said. Ken said, "She just told me that I do not have to eat anymore." She responded that I was, indeed, a very wise woman. In that moment, I realized I had given him what he needed from me—permission to die. He couldn't end this without us doing it together, and I had almost missed the sign.

I remember our wedding vows, when we promised each other before God to have and to hold from this day forward, for better or for worse, for richer or for poorer, in sickness and in health, to love and to cherish till death do us part, according to God's holy ordinance, and thereto we gave each other our troth. These were our wedding vows, and now, as our life together was coming to an end, I was being asked to release him back to God and let him go. It was the hardest thing I had ever been asked to do. He asked to be allowed to sleep away until his end. He was right, he was all done, and now he needed to let God take him when the moment was right.

He has stopped eating and only sips water and bits of ice cubes. The same palliative doctor came in a bit later to tell him that she would be off for the weekend but would be back on Tuesday morning. She sat on his bed and in her warm, easy manner shared her weekend plans. She did some medical observations, and then, as she was nearing the door to leave, she turned and smiled and said, "See you on Tuesday." Ken thanked her for all her caring of him and added, "But I won't be here when you come back, doctor."

"Oh, I am sure you will," she said as she left. But a moment later, she came back and said, "Well, then, I will see you on the other side!"

What wisdom, what empathy, what kindness! For although we know not the hour or the day, in our hearts we know that we have begun the vigil of death.

Evelyn and Mark were going to Qualicum but changed their minds, which I find myself feeling grateful for. David is out for dinner, and Jake and Heather are in the city, so I am about to have a quiet and peaceful night here with Ken. This is the first part of our "watch and pray." I sit and I read and I pray and I rest, all in the sure knowledge that this is the way it should be. Although alone, we are not apart. Rather, we knit into the lives of those we love and care for. I pray that I will have the sufficiency for the moments ahead. I pray that I will be for Ken all that he needs and that I will honour the Lord in this hard and maybe long and painful journey. I am not happy, but I am grateful that I know the joy of the Lord.

The night of the prayer vigil was powerful yet peaceful. I prayed all the prayers and psalms from the Prayer Book for the sick and for the dying. In the chapel of our church, people had come together and were holding a prayer vigil for him. So in these two places, the aroma of prayer transcended, uniting into one, as we held the light of Christ before the closing eyes of one of His beloved. Finally, as the morning took over from the night, I held him and sang lullabies, for in that moment he had become my child and I was holding him even unto death.

As morning transpired, silence was the only language I had. All the prayers, the committals, the soothing songs were finished. In that place of holy quiet, I heard words being said into my heart, words that were clear and strong: "And from this moment on, I shall be your husband and you shall know my name, for it is the Lord of Hosts." I knew them to be words of God and from scripture, but it wasn't until I was at home later that I found their origin. Into the fog of my exhaustion and sorrow came clarity:

God in His graciousness would not let me feel forsaken, nor would I be alone.

Monday, May 24

The time we usually arose from bed to begin our day was the moment Ken breathed his last breath. No matter how prepared you are, death has a shocking finality. Yet there was still a mountain I had not seen, a battle I had not fought, and that was the final letting go. That's where I was, and I could not see beyond it. The family had been alerted; Evelyn did all this. I was just numb. I hardly knew how they got there—they were just there.

We sat in a circle around his bed, without a sound. Silence is a powerful communicator. It held us together in a way that words have no power to do, allowing the shock to settle upon our heavy hearts. I have no idea how long we sat in this cocoon. I have no sense of time beyond this moment.

Gradually, I noticed slight movement from my son-in-law, as well as Jake. There was great gentleness in what they were doing. They were both looking at me, but I didn't know what was happening. As they were both doctors, they would be the ones to take him to the morgue. It was time for the rest of us to leave. I was totally unprepared for this. In my experience at other deaths, I would have left by now and this would have just happened, but now it was I who had to release him and move on. This was the final farewell.

I closed my eyes and went deep into myself, as if descending into an elevator shaft down to my deepest inner being. There I wrestled with letting go, and gradually, in an awful anguish, I released him to God. That moment of sheer agony went beyond the bounds of time.

I came back slowly from this ordeal, and then made sure Ken had his special blanket, which a dear friend had spent ages quilting for him, as well as a special pillow that he loved. He never went anywhere without that pillow. I couldn't let him go unless he was warm and covered before I kissed him goodbye. I pleaded with the boys to make sure that the undertaker knew to keep him tucked in the blanket and his head on the pillow. I knew this was not rational, but I didn't care. I was frantic to continue caring for him, to make sure he was tucked in and loved. They promised. The undertaker told me just before the funeral, as the coffin was waiting to go into the church, that they had followed all my instructions. Ken was safe and warm. The mind and heart do not need sense or reason; they need love and compassion. I knew he didn't need these things. It was I who needed them, and this was the final thing I could do for him. It was my surge of protective love.

I don't remember going home, except that Evelyn drove me. At first my children were there; then it was time for me to be alone. The first thing I did was to research the words I had heard in the hospital. I needed to find the verse of scripture, and discovered it was from the Book of Isaiah chapter 54, verse 5. I was comforted by how exact the words were to what I had heard. Their clarity and accuracy confirmed once again the reality, the love and the intentionality of God. Next, I wrote in my calendar, "This morning at 7:15, my darling died." I was about to begin the journey without him.

I don't think we are ever prepared for these moments. Academically we can know, but the head and heart need to travel together, and that takes time. I remember walking upstairs to my office, past the hall table that held all the family photos. I could hear Ken's voice as clear as day saying, "Don't look, don't look," as he always did when he saw something that would upset me. I could not look at a picture of him—it would have destroyed me. It was his voice calling me out of danger. It would be many months before I could look at a photo of him, or of us together.

The next hurdle was to shower and change before Evelyn and Mark came over to share a glass of wine. Only upon reflection did I realize that this was my first conscious decision to move forward. Walking into that shower took huge discipline. I remember it clearly. It took energy, and yes, I would even say courage, to strip myself of my hospital clothes and walk away from them. Putting them down purposefully and moving into the cleansing shower would become a symbol of my choice to live and move forward. It was costly, but it was also my choice to listen to God my Husband, who was calling me forth.

It has been said that faith is the step between promise and assurance. I believe in God's promise that He is who He says He is, and that He will continue to give me the assurance of remaining faithful to that promise. He is there, He will be there and He will remain there. Yet, why is faith so hard?

What came next is what every family goes through: the need to notify, to talk, to plan the next step. Ken had organized everything. Together, we had planned his funeral and all the arrangements, so I knew what was expected. Even so, it seemed that my feet were held in cement. Nothing worked properly, and everything that had been so clear was now foreign and beyond my capacity to cope.

Evelyn was my go-to person. She phoned the family, did all the necessary connecting. To this day, I do not know how she did it. She must have paid a dear price. I relied on her for so much. Everyone helped, but she was the true north in this storm of loss. I will never forget her love and kindness. There is no script for this play called death, no lines for you to learn. You either do it or you don't. It is either within you or it is not.

We did so much that I cannot remember. Everything up to this time remains crystal clear, but the period before his funeral is shrouded. Alerting and conversing with those who would speak was huge and was being done, but mostly by rote or just by doing. Then there were the funeral plans, the bulletin, the flowers, organizing the pallbearers, the sidesmen, the music, the food. Our dear friend Lyn was coming from Colorado to be with me, a blessing. Family was arriving from the east, and David's family was coming from London. By the Grace of God and little else, I somehow moved forward.

Friday, May 28, 2010

Today is the day of the funeral. Lyn has arrived and I am grateful for her quiet, solid presence. She and I will go to the church together, and the rest of the family will meet in the library before the service. Everything is in place. The flowers are in the church, and the ushers and pallbearers are organized. Now it is just a matter of getting through it all. The bulletins were specially printed, and on the front is a picture of Ken and MacGregor. It is a lovely photograph.

Some of the funeral is a blur, but I clearly remember Rod's speech. Rod was with us at the beginning of this last chapter of our lives, and he has remained, as always, a faithful friend and companion. Ken wanted Rod to speak at his funeral, and so Rod came over one Saturday morning to visit and find out what Ken wanted him to say. Ken was clear about what he wanted, and they discussed this in a relaxed and comfortable way. If someone who didn't know the circumstances had been listening, they would have thought that Rod and Ken were planning a seminar, discussing what was to be said, the scriptures, the thoughts, the desires, and how best to honour the Lord.

When Rod left that morning, Ken turned to me and said, "I would love to hear what Rod is going to do with this, what he will say." Then he asked, "Are you going to have this recorded?"

"I'd never thought of that. I don't know if it is necessary," I said.

"Yes," he said, "do record it, and when you come, bring it with you." The almost childlike reality of his still clear and brilliant mind was touching and beautiful.

I told this to Rod, and at the funeral when he had finished his sermon, he held up his notes and said, "Gail, I sincerely hope that you will not be leaving us for quite some time, but when you go, take this with you." It felt like Paul's second letter to Timothy in the final chapter, where he says to Timothy, "Do your best to get here before winter; when you come, bring the cloak that I left with Carpus at Troas, and my scrolls, especially the parchments."

Our dear friend Eggy was the perfect bookend for all that was said at Ken's service. He told of who Ken was as a person and illustrated it with personal stories. These two men were beautiful gifts.

Evelyn read a poem that I had written to Ken for our fiftieth wedding anniversary. He always carried it with him and had asked her to read it at the funeral. It broke my heart to listen to her heart-wrenching reading. She was a picture of bravery.

The service was beautiful, honouring God and re-membering Ken well, and soon it was over. As we recessed to "Amazing Grace" played by the bagpipes, I realized that there is always more to these events than you think about. Ken's casket had to be put into the hearse. He was leaving now, and we were moving on. Again, it was like standing on the shoreline watching a ship depart. The ship is leav-ing and you are not going with it. It evokes every emotion in your body and soul, and yet I had to move on. There was still the reception, where we would meet people, and they were waiting.

As a family, we had agreed that there would be a few words spoken at the beginning of the reception. My Bible study group had taken on pouring the tea and manag-ing the tea tables. It had been beautifully catered, and I was grateful for how attractive and welcoming the church hall looked. The poster that Ken's Bible study group had made for him in the hospital was hanging on the wall, and there were flowers everywhere, as well as the glow of many candles.

In planning this part of the funeral, it was agreed that if I could manage to speak, then I would speak last. That way, there would be no awkward moment if I felt I could not. It wasn't until I was on my feet that I knew I would be able to speak.

I started by telling everyone how much Ken had wanted me to thank them for all their love and care, for their prayers as well as their concerns. I told them how often he had mentioned that even in his isolation, he felt the community and connection. He was grateful for all the love and the many things that everyone had done to keep him feeling connected. This meant so much, because they were alive to him all through his journey. I mentioned the Bible study poster, the emails, the notes, the thoughtful items of food, but most importantly the love, the care and the prayers. Through all of this, it was clear that being present can happen in deep ways even when we are separated physically. He felt this in his being, and it was important that I convey to everyone how grateful and deeply blessed he felt.

I then read what I had written about gratitude, such a significant factor these past four months. These may have been my words, but they were his thoughts, and it mat-

tered to him that these words of gratitude and remember-
ing be said to those who had so faithfully held the candle
of light, hope and love through his months of preparing
for death.

My memory of the reception is mostly about the peo-
ple and their conversations. There was great warmth and
caring. I was overwhelmed by the number of people who
came to Ken's funeral, and by their presence I was blessed.
I was surprised at how much this meant to me. I needed
him to be well remembered. He was not someone who
wished recognition, but it soothed my soul to see how
respected and beloved he was.

I shall never forget Colin Campbell, who came up
to me quietly at the reception and said, "3389 reporting
in." This was his military number from Royal Military
College. I was able to reply that on behalf of 3427, I was
receiving him with great delight! His gentle strength was a
gift I will always treasure.

There were also dear friends who had come from
Eastern Canada and the United States. I cannot thank
all these precious people enough for their gift of love.
Through your caring, you created a perfume of love that
will linger in my heart forever. To all of you—thank you!

Our children were wonderful, with their solid dignity
and strength. This must have been so hard for them. Ken
was their father, their rock. I saw them interacting, greet-

ing people, being upheld by their own friends, but above all just being the people they are.

When the reception was over, the family and a few close friends went to Evelyn and Mark's home for dinner. It was beautifully done, but I had no energy left and was the first to leave after dinner. Dear Lyn and I went home, she the tower of strength and I, by this time, limp with exhaustion. I was grateful for the gift of the funeral, for the love and support of all the people, for the solidarity of our family. Now that it was over, for a short time there was nothing more I could do. It was finished and a new chapter lay waiting for me. From now on, everything would be different.

I thought of the prayer that Ken and I had said every evening together, how we always remembered to find something to be grateful for. There was gratitude in my heart for the goodness of the Lord, for what He had done, for the family I have and for the sweetness of love. Until morning, I was going to commit all of this to the Lord and slip into what I prayed would be a peaceful sleep.

∽

O Lord, support us all the day long
of this troublous life,
until the shadows lengthen
and the evening comes,
the busy world is hushed,
the fever of life is over,
and our work is done.
Then Lord, in thy mercy,
grant us safe lodging,
a holy rest,
and peace at the last;
through Jesus Christ our Lord.
Amen
(Book of Common Prayer, 1962)

Part III

Reflections on Grieving

Photo by Beverly Wilson

It has been said that the storms of life are best understood when they have sufficiently subsided. So it is with the journey called grief. It was only when the turbulence was over that I could see with some clarity the depth and anguish of what had happened. I needed time to make sense of what I could not fully understand when the waters were churning. Now that Ken was gone, I felt as if my pen had run dry and my heart had fractured, but I was grateful to see God's steady and encouraging hand as I continued along this long and painful path of grief.

I thought I was prepared for the process of mourning, yet it felt as if a stranger had assaulted the intimacy of my heart. The most intense moments arrived without warning, filling my space and leaving me breathless and exhausted. Sometimes a heavy fog shrouded all sense of direction and reason, leaving me lost, confused and overwhelmed. Though it has been nearly four years, I still feel the pain and loss, but God's deep, abiding love continues to hold my heart steady, keeping me from stumbling and falling.

During the period of Ken's dying, he often said, "Thank you for doing for me what I cannot do." He could not imagine being the one left behind, and he was grateful that he wasn't being asked to do this work. His gratitude was a precious gift of love, but I would have preferred that the roles be reversed, that I was the one leaving rather than being left.

Although he was concerned for those who remained, he was never afraid of dying. He spoke of it as a wonderful journey to Heaven, where he would be with the Lord, waiting for me. He reminded me that this was just a moment in time and he wasn't leaving me; he was just going ahead. Perhaps that is why we never really said goodbye. It would always remain "until then."

Grief was not unfamiliar to me, yet this loss felt as new and raw as anything I could ever imagine. Even though I had lost my parents and many dear people I loved, even though in my pastoral ministry I had walked alongside people whose lives were affected by illness, sorrow and loss, I was unprepared for this storm of pain. But God in His love and wisdom sent me what I needed. He gave me deep awareness of Himself and reminded me to remember. All through scripture, we are reminded again and again to remember. We remember in the breaking of bread and the drinking of wine during Holy Communion. We are invited to "Do this in remembrance of me." So as I walked my journey, I reflected on what I had learned from the journeys of others. And again they became my teachers. They taught me how to read a question locked in the heart, how to watch and pray and not interrupt God's work. They reminded me of the vital need to be a midwife for the soul. It was from them that I learned that each death and loss, although always different, could be a holy birth, that an undivided heart, even when broken, remains holy ground. I learned that we all need empathy, love and acceptance more than direction and advice.

Yet, in spite of all the guides I had and all I had learned, at times it was still a confusing and lonely road. Grief and mourning can feel like emotional hobbles, restraining and holding you as you attempt to walk this slow and messy journey, often all alone, creating a strange isolation.

When I was a young girl, my wise mother continually taught me to walk in others' shoes so that I would understand their journey. But for most people, the journey of loss and grief is fraught with confusion—we do not know how to do this. How do you walk in someone's shoes when you have no idea of their pain? And how does the one grieving reach out with arms too weary to extend to others? In his book *Letters from the Land of Cancer*, Walter Wangerin Jr. reminded me anew of this valuable lesson when he wrote, "I now put myself in the shoes of those who feel unable to put themselves in mine." He, who had always been the caregiver, had to learn to help those who did not know how to walk alongside him in his illness.

His words were a message of encouragement to me, as I was finding that most people struggled to walk in the uncomfortable shoes I was now wearing. I slowly discovered that the eye can only see what it is shown, and this abbreviated form of myself actually created discomfort for some people. I became aware that people in deep grief often seem to embrace others or retreat from them. This is a reaction to pain, not to the person who is trying to assist, but sometimes this reaction can cause them distress.

My journey was complicated by a heart problem, making it even more difficult for others to walk alongside me. Upon reflection I realize that my loss of health was a gift of time that God gave me to adjust to the loss and prepare for the work that lay ahead. Through some of the difficult times, God in His wisdom sent me angels over and over again. Some were able to walk with me in the moment, and by their very presence they encouraged me to carry on. Others came disguised in ways that I did not recognize, but slowly, as I dealt with this loss, God began to reveal the secret of His loving care.

Recently, I found myself remembering my first major loss. My maternal grandfather died when I was twelve years old. It was my first real encounter with death. My grandfather had emigrated from Scotland to Canada and carried within himself a strong moral code of conduct. He was responsible, committed to his family and his work, and without doubt the most internally disciplined person I have ever met. His life deeply impacted my own. I heard how brave he was as he struggled with cancer, but I did not understand what suffering, pain, death or loss were all about. Although his death was anticipated, and my grandmother, mother and father walked with him through the period of his dying, I had no idea what the finality of death was like.

I can still remember the quiet shock the night he died. I had a sense of having nowhere to go, that all my safe places were gone. I felt lost and sad and helpless as my family prepared for his funeral. The funeral was a holy sacrament, providing a place for everyone to gather. I remember how my family acted and what they did before and after the funeral. I understood very little at the time, but now I realize these moments were the foundation for learning how families go through death and dying.

In the cultural mores of the time, there was a structure holding the brokenness and helping direct us through the morass of pain and loss. Often, black crepe was draped across the front door, or a black wreath was hung at the entrance of the deceased's home. Men wore black ties and armbands, and women wore all black. This dress code defined mourning, and how long the mourning lasted was decreed by your relationship with the deceased. Often, women of the family wore grey for the following year.

All of this has changed so quickly, and perhaps radically, since my grandparents' time that we seem to have lost many patterns and points of reference. The outward symbols that gave messages to people are now gone, and the topic of death is avoided. I think that grieving people are intuitively aware that they are causing discomfort for others. Not wanting to burden anyone with our pain, we try to get through it as quickly as possible and get back into the world we know and understand. This makes it difficult to do the work of grief or find a wise mentor to guide us.

I wonder if by not knowing what to say or do, we are denying comfort to the dying person, who may feel that they are letting the team down, that they are a burden. They often have nowhere to go where they are free to discuss their fears or anxieties, and they do not want to add pain to their families and friends. Even the medical profession is unable to help, as it is overextended and in some cases underqualified.

I believe there is great sadness when we forget that God so desires to gather His children to Himself, to comfort and heal the broken-hearted. God, who is in every moment, encourages and yearns for us to enter into these moments with Him. He invites the dying into the intimacy and dignity of life through the acceptance of death. It can be a place of freedom to tell stories, as well as an opportunity to say I love you, to remember and to plan together.

I remember Ken saying several times, as he approached the time of death, how little it mattered what success he may have achieved. He said no one remembers what you have done, but they will remember who you were, the words you spoke and if you loved well. I hold in my heart memory the many times he said, "I love you," especially one beautiful moment just hours before his death. As I tucked him into his hospital bed, wearied with grief, he looked up into my eyes and said, "You are so beautiful." Such are the eyes of love!

As I continue to walk this journey of grief and remember the loss, I am deeply aware of God the parent, God the husband, God the lover, and God the friend who walks with me. I am reminded that in this place, where options appear to have been removed and only the vast void of the unknown faces me, I do have choices. I can see the door of death as a holy passing or a harsh slam in the face.

God, who is in my history and my present, draws me to look more clearly into the calmer waters so I can focus on the beauty rather than the pain. I choose to remember the wonderful life Ken and I were granted. Although I still feel the loss, and there is not a day that I do not miss him, I see more deeply God's hand upon everything.

Occasionally I still feel very alone, and yet there is always the presence of God yearning to speak into the heart of His beloved. I believe that the mystery of God is His very closeness. God's powerful presence is His knowing our pain and our hearts, for He is "a man of sorrows, and acquainted with grief" (Isaiah 53:3b KJV). I am continually learning that I need to be very still to know the quiet presence of God's love and let words of prayer, as the language of His love, speak into my heart and my soul.

None of us knows the hour of our death, and I feel that God yearns for us to spend more time living intentionally and loving fully. I believe that what we say and do has far more effect than we may ever know, as our lives are deeply woven into the fabric of others. Our memory of God's goodness encourages the heart to be grateful and to know that the gift of love lives on and the story continues long after the last breath is taken.

Ken and I were blessed to live a love story, and that story is neither lost nor over. A life well lived and a life well loved is a treasure that will last forever. My prayer is that it will become more precious now that it is shared, and it may become a love story for others.

As I walk farther on in my journey, I continue to learn and I am at peace. I live in the hope and sure anticipation that we have a wonderful future ahead of us. I am claiming the truth that all things will be made new and we will see each other again. How much do I love you, my darling? Forever. Until then, my darling, until then.

What no eye has seen
   what no ear has heard
   and what no human mind has conceived—
   the things God has prepared for those who love
him.
   (1 Corinthians 2:9)

Part IV

Poetic Prayers of Reflection

On Becoming

The powerful voice of God
speaks gently into
the silence of my heart
turning my inner chaos
into rays of hope,
changing darkness into light.

In the stillness of my being
my eyes begin to see,
in the quietness of my soul
my heart begins to understand
that through His gentle power,
gradually I become.

Why Do I Pray?

I pray because I need to pray.
I pray because I believe
God is calling me to Himself.
I yearn to respond
even when there are no words.

Prayer gives me peace
when God speaks
into the heart of His beloved.

Prayer is the breath of life
into the place of despair.
Prayer is more
than a word of comfort
or a sign of hope.
It is life-shaping and life-changing.

Prayer is that connection,
that rope of hope.
It is the tangible amidst the chaos,
it is the quiet and the small
in the enormity of pain.
It is the something bigger and better
than the breaking of my heart.

It is knowing that
in the vortex of suffering,
God is not only present,
He is holding,
He is rescuing,
He is receiving me
even unto death.

Faith and prayer are not
a drowning gasp of hope,
but a seizing of the firm mast of God's truth
amidst life's turbulent waters.
It is there and it is real
and I need to hold it hard and tight.

Wrestling with God

Like Jacob
I have wrestled through the
dark night of my pain.

Like Jacob
I have asked
for a blessing and a new name.

I no longer ask the why
but rather the how.

I pray that God in His mercy
will reach down and
touch my lips
and give me the words to say.

A Prayer of Commitment

I come naked, Oh Lord,
offering who I am to You.

Alone without excuse
I stand,
offering my nothingness
in exchange for Your
everything.

I commit myself to You
knowing that only Your Holiness
can clothe eternity.

Amen

Seasons of My Soul

Holy, holy, holy,
everything is holy.

Darkness and sunlight,
rain, hail and snow,
all of it is holy.

Lord God Almighty,
gatherer of the seasons,
guardian of my soul,
grant me small
glimpses of
ordinary holiness.

God in Motion

When God chooses to move,
when God lifts His hand,
His voice thunders,
breaking the silence
stretching across
endless barriers of time.

Those insurmountable moments are,
in one moment,
in one thrust,
shattered, scattered,
rendered, redone,
made new, redefined,
a new creation.

Just one word
and we are transformed.

A Prayer for Sustenance

Heavenly Father,
I pray that You
who have created life
will sustain and keep it,
keeping all that is good,
all that is loved,
all that is lost.

I pray that You
prepare and create
in me a desire
to prepare and create
for You
a ready dwelling place.

Amen

Prayer at Night Time

In the middle of the night
the clock chimes
into the still silence.

It reminds me
that in the midst of rest
and sleep
time moves on,
things do change
and life balances
as the earth journeys on—

Yet You, God,
in Your mercy,
instruct my heart
so I can move into
the safety of Your being.

You cradle me
in the midst of things
I cannot change
as time moves on
relentlessly
through the
middle of the night.

Prayer of Hope

O Lord my God,
safe in the shadow of Your wings,
I offer You the prayer of hope
that You will support me
when I am little
and when I am old.

For when my strength
springs from me,
it is weakness,
but when it is only from You
it is real strength.

Leaning upon You
I can find my way back
to You,
You who are my refreshment
and my true strength.

Amen

The Kaleidoscope of Change

Christ is in the business
of making all things new;
like a kaleidoscope
we are being turned
as we watch and see
new ways, new thoughts,
always being transformed
into something
new and beautiful
for God.

The Pain of Loss

There is a pain
that speaks such words
as cannot be uttered.

There is a pain
that transcends all
feeling and thought.

A pain that binds
our hearts to
the heart of God,
and holds us in
the hearts of one another.

In the silence
of love
we simply are.

Two Chairs

Two chairs
facing each other,
two people
moving slowly together
as they
listen in silence,
gradually creating
a space
for the
mind and heart
to speak
the language
of love,
mixing
compassion and healing
together,
allowing God
the alchemist
to pour Himself
into the creation
of a family.

Prayer of Solitude

I have found you at last,
my beloved ocean.
With you, I am alone
with no agenda, no expectations,
just the simplicity of being,
to hear again your stillness,
to feel your quietness,
to absorb and to savour
your taste and scent
and your colour.

Such a vast intimacy,
so precious, so perfect.

By your very nature
you are so near
and yet so far away.
You give an energy
both quiet and raucous,
yet you hold your beloved
in powerful tenderness.

For all that you are,
I can never hold on to you.
I can only experience,
through you,
the wonderful mystery of life.

Gratitude

I believe that
gratitude is made
authentic by being
able to say
thank you, Lord,
before the
finished results.

I believe that
gratitude is true
when we know
that God is with us
in the beginning,
the centre,
and will be at the end.

I believe that
gratitude is ours
when we can unite
with Jesus in
the midst of the
fearfully unknown
and find ourselves
being found
in Him
who is our all.

That is my gratitude.

The Gift of Gratitude

Lord,
I pray that
I may see life as a gift
for then
I will have seen God.

I pray that
I may see beauty
in people and in things
for then
I will have seen the divine.

I pray that
I may value what is good
and honour what is holy
for then
I will have known gratitude.

Amen

Goodbye

There is nothing so awful
and yet so simple
as saying goodbye.
There is nothing more final
or heartbreaking
than death.

Yet death is simple —
a moving from pain to glory,
from a time of life to
life for eternity.

It is so simple because
it is of God.
It is so painful
because we know only
in part what we will
soon know in full.

While we in our humanity
still suffer such pain,
God in His holiness
hold us and weeps
His love into our hearts.

Angel Wings

You have to be very still
to hear the whisper of angel wings,
to be touched by nature's
symphonic sounds
that move the silent heart
into a dance of joy.

You have to be very still
to become.

Afterword

Many of our conversations during the latter part of my husband Ken's life included his desire to thank everyone who had ministered to and cared for him through the last four months of his life. One day he asked me to write something that I could read at the reception following his funeral service.

He wanted to thank all the people who had taken so much time and thought in preparing and delivering the wonderful morsels of food, the casseroles, the notes of encouragement and heartfelt emotion; the loving hands that made and delivered the exquisite quilt; all those who prayed without ceasing; those who sent flowers; and the dear friends who looked after our dogs. These were some of the tangible ways that manifested the often-intangible word "love."

Ken asked me to tell everyone how much it had meant to him, that in spite of his isolation, his heart had seen the width and breadth of their care. This was especially important to him because he could not express these words himself.

But like the letter of gratitude to his philanthropic friend who made possible the palliative wing in the hospital, the thought of standing up and speaking loomed before me as an impossible task. I was amazed that he would even entertain such a thought, but this was clearly important and he was asking me to speak for him. This was a man who throughout our whole married life had protected and cared for me, like the eagle's extended wing, so great was the power and strength of that love. Yet, it never entered his mind that I would have any difficulty with his last request, as it was simply what we had always done. As the Lord met Jeremiah, I prayed that the Lord would reach out and touch my mouth and give me the words to say.

The words of "Gratitude" that follow are the ones I read at the reception after I spoke about our desire to thank everyone. Now, today, I again dedicate these words to all the wonderful angels of mercy who walked beside me when I could not walk in my own shoes. You are too many to name, but your many names are forever written within my heart.

જી

Gratitude cannot become an active word unless it has been birthed out of the depths of suffering and into a new understanding.

Gratitude is an active word involving every part of our being, transforming acceptance, forgiveness and awareness.

Gratitude actively seeks to see the hand of God in adversity, and then watches and prays as a miracle takes place: eventually pain can become a blessing, agony a joy, and loss a gain.

Gratitude in suffering is to risk walking into the unknown with the known God. It is risking our control to His divine purpose and allowing our failures and losses to be transformed into something beautiful for God.

I am grateful for all that the Lord has done. I stand here today deeply humbled yet overwhelmed with the pain of loss, but with a greater sense of awe and worship for the God who continually comes in our most lonely and abandoned moments, granting us grace upon grace and surprising and delighting us with joy!

Today I especially thank the Lord for all His gracious love, and I thank you, dear friends, for all your love and support.

Thank you.

Gail Stevenson

May 28, 2010

Acknowledgments

I want to thank Heather Doty, without whom
this journal would never have reached
the edited stage,

Joyce Gram,
who did the final editing,

and my sister and brothers in Christ,
Irene, Jim and Rod,
who read with discerning hearts.

CPSIA information can be obtained at www.ICGtesting.com
Printed in the USA
LVOW02s2318170714

394839LV00002B/5/P